Translated by Howard Scott

# This Could Be Anywhere

Maude Smith Gagnon

BookLand press

French-language edition published by Les Éditions Triptyque



Published by BookLand Press
15 Allstate Parkway, Suite 600, Markham, Ontario L3R 5B4
www.booklandpress.com

Printed and bound in Canada

Front cover image © Jill Battaglia | Dreamstime.com

**Library and Archives Canada Cataloguing in Publication**

Smith Gagnon, Maude, 1980-
[Un drap, une place. English]

This could be anywhere / Maude Smith Gagnon; translated by Howard Scott.

Translation of: Un drap, une place.
Poems.
Winner of the Governor General's Award for French-language poetry.
Issued in print and electronic formats.
ISBN 978-1-926956-83-1 (pbk.).--ISBN 978-1-926956-84-8 (epub).--
ISBN 978-1-926956-85-5 (pdf)
I. Scott, Howard, 1952-, translator II. Title. III. Title: Un drap, une place. English

PS8637.M5695D7213 2014    C841'.6    C2013-907217-9
C2013-907218-7

Canada Council for the Arts | Conseil des arts du Canada

ONTARIO ARTS COUNCIL
CONSEIL DES ARTS DE L'ONTARIO
50 YEARS OF ONTARIO GOVERNMENT SUPPORT OF THE ARTS
50 ANS DE SOUTIEN DU GOUVERNEMENT DE L'ONTARIO AUX ARTS

We acknowledge the financial support of the Government of Canada, through the National Translation Program for Book Publishing for our translation activities. We acknowledge the support of the Canada Council for the Arts, which last year invested $157 million to bring the arts to Canadians throughout the country. We acknowledge the support of the Ontario Arts Council (OAC), an agency of the Government of Ontario, which last year funded 1,681 individual artists and 1,125 organizations in 216 communities across Ontario for a total of $52.8 million.

*Why this need. You should know that yesterday, for example, I sat down on a concrete block, that it started to rain and I stayed there, just looking at what was in front of me. A street, a building and a door, with people going in or going out.*

# Table of Contents

# *Natashquan*

## June 7

On the ground near the big building, an old tarpaulin, a woodpile and puddles stretched by the wind. Long empty hours opened up before me and, not necessarily to fill them, I watch Serge tidying up the yard. For the last few days he hasn't been able to find his scarf. Instead, he tied a dishtowel around his neck. You don't write to me much. The weather here is a pale grey. Same sky as yesterday, but lower. I don't watch it for very long.

## June 18

It's raining on the sea. And the waves, as they swell, carry off the orange juice carton that I'm trying to catch with a long stick.

## June 13

At the bottom of a hill, near a big rock, I spotted two empty Yum Yum bags this morning. This image came to me: the two of us, side by side, our pants wet with dew. We eat chips without a word, watching the shadows of the bushes sliding down the slope. In the distance, the sea and the sky. Two blues that don't go together, it seemed, that day.

## *August 14*

The trees bend, straighten up, then bend again. I walk, holding in my hand a piece of paper picked up somewhere. My tracks in the sand fill with water.

## June 27

I'd like to talk to you about that moment. It was around noon. I was sitting in the kitchen, my chin resting in the hollow of my hand. I observed the table and its turquoise wash, my backpack, the brown cup, the tea rings, the crumbled cellophane. None of this, except for the turquoise of the table, occupied a central place in my field of vision. The outlines of objects were still partially vague. For long, long minutes (one or two actually, but it's easy to say that now) I stared at this insignificant portion of my universe, as if hypnotized, unable to elude it when it would have been so simple to lift my head, look outside and say anything – "it smells bad," for example, which was true – or move on to something else. I don't know why I'm writing all this. Since this morning, the air has been damp. My fingernails are dirty. I don't need you to find me interesting, not today.

# *May 10*

Two light bulbs hang over the bed on a single wire. The room still gets a little brightness. From the bowl sitting between my legs, I pick out a soft grape.

## May 22

The shadows on the wall have changed. At the foot of the bed, the clock face gives off a green light.

# July 15

Jean-Lou plans to stay for a few more days. Every night on the doorstep, he watches us disappear in the distance with our thermoses. At first, I didn't understand what he meant exactly when he asked, "Where's my friend?" Later I learned that during our absence, he spent a lot of his time playing with Margarine, the little cat.

## *July 3*

Behind the rows of blue chairs, there's a wall and a sign hanging from wires. I stand up and go sit down a little farther away, on a flat rock that is neither big or small, from where I can see the wharf and the almost motionless boats.

## *July 31*

It's not dark yet, but the sun is gone. A windless evening. In places, the clouds come loose.

## August 11

The first thing that comes to mind as I'm crossing the street is that air is going into my lungs. For an instant, the centre of my chest seems to me like a place, strangely vast and impersonal. For no reason, I look at my watch, then the clouds. A big white expanse that doesn't move.

## July 29

Outside, it's grey. Rainwater swamps the grass in the yard. Lunch.

# August 7

At the back of the restaurant, a couple sits down. All the tables between us are unoccupied. The man takes off his coat, lays it over the back of his chair. Even sitting down, he looks tall. His hair, long and black, contrasts with his pale eyes. As he speaks, the woman rolls up a paper serviette to make a bracelet. She looks outside. It's still raining.

# Vietnam

# *May 11*

There is a wall with two windows. Each one looks out on the same thing: trees.

## May 21

Light comes into the room. It warms my left arm, not the right. On the ceiling, a reflection quivers.

## May 12

Through the dirty window, there are trees and trees. I see them go by one after the other, aware that none of them will be part of my memory. The bus is moving fast. Behind me, someone opens a package, other people are talking about things I don't understand. A man stands up, looks at the road ahead, then sits down again. We are crossing a valley. Then more big trees appear, and it continues like this for a very long time.

## *May 16*

This place is officially called "The Square." It occupies the centre of the village: open and empty, surrounded by narrow stairs that make it look like a small stadium. It doesn't look like a playing field though. Nor a place for prayer or commemoration. It's not even used as a meeting place. No one walks through it. The grass has been growing for a long time between its pale concrete flagstones.

## May 31

A woman takes a receipt from her bag and throws it to the wind. The receipt tumbles along the sidewalk, joins other papers. I observe the scene as if it were something important. I'm not really thinking about anything in particular. I'm watching the movements.

## September 9

At the time, I didn't think to tell you. It had rained all morning. I was drying my clothes in a kind of shelter made of metal posts and yellowed canvas. At my feet lay a bag and two tired dogs: a male with a golden coat and a visibly pregnant female with a pale coat. I had been told that the man who owned this piece of land beat his dogs, that one day he had even eaten them. It's possible. The man's name was Tram. He was sitting beside me. We had been talking for quite a while. About anything and everything, about the mountains in the region, about the rain, about cell phones. The clothes weren't drying fast. I finally asked him if he gave his dogs names.

"Yes," he answered, looking pleased. "That's Yellow. That's White."

## *May 31*

When I look in the rear-view mirror, silvery particles appear and disappear, in no particular order. An effect of the light. As if it had rained.

## *May 29*

Rain. Rain. It accumulates in the fields, in the hollows of leaves, on my sleeves.

## *May 14*

Spider plants hang over the mostly empty tables. A woman comes over and asks me what I'll have. I try to answer as I stare at a plant. The woman walks away and, quite a while later, returns.

# *May 15*

The man sitting near me turns and asks me a question. We gradually get into a conversation. The rays of the sun shine through the glasses sitting on the low table. I swallow a mouthful of water. The man is polite, often agreeing with what I say. Behind him, there's a plant, and a fan always blowing in the same direction.

## *June 2*

I drink broth right from the bowl, which is so big that I have to hold it in both hands. It's hot. The person sitting across from me speaks to me again. I see only the bottom of the bowl, continue drinking even though the broth no longer interests me.

## *May 28*

The wind seeps into the room, lifting the curtains. At the edge of the table, the rings of my glass are starting to disappear. I put my finger on the tip of a spoon. It reflects my face: tiny, inverted, a little deformed.

## June 1

The street is quiet. A radio can be heard somewhere, sometimes the noise of dishes.

## *May 25*

Dozing on a pier in the sunshine at four o'clock. One foot that almost touches the water. Under my eyelids, ever-changing images.

# *Montreal*

# *July 4*

The light lingers on the bouquet sitting in the centre of the table. Two stems hang over either side of the glass. I don't notice any smell. In the water, an orange label with a price floats.

## July 10

A white line, painted directly on the grass, marks the outlines of the field. I am sitting in the fifth row, the highest. The wind is puffing up my sweater. The day wanes. The bleachers are empty, the field too. My eyelids grow heavy.

## January 28

It's night. At first you see nothing. The room is silent. Familiar, but silent. Then your eyes gradually get used to the dark. With the glow from outside, you can guess the dimensions of the room, the location of furniture. No details or colours. At this stage, do you sometimes have the impression that the space in front of you is no longer really empty, that it is becoming matter you seem to be able to lean on? I can already hear you answering me: "No."

## February 5

The square of light no longer touches the table. Now it extends to my thigh and the side of the chair. It's not even a square anymore. Everything is quiet in the room. No voices. No people moving around. Just the usual street noises: cars passing, braking. I stand there, as if frozen, looking at the blue of the walls and, out the window, the gradation of the sky. This is not what I'd intended to do.

# January 29

I got into the habit of sitting down at the kitchen table one or two hours a week to learn English. Today my books are open, but my attention is elsewhere. Outside I see the snow-covered roofs, the balconies. I'm waiting for the place to open up on something other than itself, for it to make room for a memory, an image. As time passes, I still don't see anything but snowy roofs and balconies. That's probably why I'm writing to you. Most of the time I write to you when I don't know what to do, what to think about what is around me. As if the fact that I'm sharing my uneasiness could in some way bring me closer to you. This may not be the case.

## October 21

Out the bathroom window, through the toothpaste splatters, I observe the irregular line of the roofs, the wind in the trees. A taste of mint warms my gums.

## January 13

There is a rope around the damaged section of the balcony. You barely notice it, mostly hear it, flapping in the wind. The window I'm writing in front of lets in a breath of air. On the roofs dazzling strips of snow. The sky behind them does not dazzle. It is pale, without depth.

## February 7

A few rare red coats in the crowd, under big clouds that cast shadows over everything. Voices blend with the noise of wet soles. I listen to snatches of conversation. At the end of the street, the overpass begins to appear. A row of newly planted trees extends almost continually to it. I stop for a moment at the curb to tie my shoe. I haven't taken advantage of the sun much lately.

## *May 24*

It's not really because of the late hour. Or because of the solitude, I don't think so. The walls, the black windows, the smooth floors: something in their presence is not enough, is not familiar to me. Something somehow is missing. All I notice, as the minutes tick by, is the uniformity of this absence.

## November 2

The clouds look like a big mattress today. White dominates. I look in front of me: the trees with their empty branches, the sheet stretched on the line since yesterday, stiffened by the cold. I imagine this same scene seen from somewhere else, from another balcony, or from a roof. The shapes and colours change, just barely. The sound of water now holds my attention. For an instant I see Niagara Falls.

## July 17

The notebook looked handmade. Thick, poorly cut pages, bound with transparent thread. I had found it, a few years ago, at the bottom of a box and had opened it up at random. At the bottom of one of the pages, which were a little hard to turn, were the words:

"On the paths of life
Be my light
Hallelu Hallelu Hallelu Hallelujah."

Today, for whatever reason, those words came back to me: "Hallelu Hallelu Hallelu Hallelujah." I try to imagine what melody they were sung to. I can't.

## November 16

The woman's name was Annie. She was tired. You could see it in her absent smile, in the way she said her words. She received me in her office just before five o'clock. Just as I was about to sit down, the phone rang. She excused herself before answering the call, then she barely paid attention to me. I didn't dare take off my tuque or my coat.

I never saw that woman again. But I still have the image of pink, green and blue photocopies lying around her office. I see the phone that she held in the crook of her shoulder, the big clock above her head. I see her laugh, then adjust the sleeve of her dress. Above all, I see myself, as she must have seen me at that moment. That is, as a person of about thirty years of age who is waiting.

# *November 24*

The tree, with the sky behind it. The unoccupied table. The compact brown of the soil. This moment reminds me of no particular memory. My gaze moves from one thing to another, bands of light rippling on the ground with its snowy park benches.

## *September 12*

Inside a car, a woman is reading or waiting. I lean towards her and ask her where Jean-Talon Street is. It's not a prepared question. I don't know why I'm asking her that. The woman takes a few seconds to answer. She's tying her long hair back, and I imagine what she'd look like without it.

# May 19

The vacant lot, a year ago, was covered with brush and bleached grass. That winter there had been almost no snow. In the mud, the tracks of feet and trucks accumulated; the frost had frozen them. I can still see Thomas standing behind the hedge that separated the lot from the street. Only his forehead and eyebrows were visible. I remember saying something nice to him. I couldn't see his face, but I think he smiled. At the foot of the hedge the grass held the light. It was cold. I didn't feel like going home.

# January 8

The snow occupies the entire width of the street. It gathers on bicycle frames, along fences. I walk along the sidewalk more slowly than usual. Dryer vents fill the air with a smell that doesn't match what my eyes see.

## *March 9*

I'd like it if everything I see today out my window vanished, if the walls fell, if there were no longer around me a smooth expanse where the wind blows.

It could be a beach. Nothing to block the view, only the line of the water and perhaps in the distance the line of the coast.

The beach covered in snow. Broken ice making the waves pale, as they break heavily two feet from my boots. On the wind smells of iodine and clay. Streaks of sand dirtying the snow in places.

Instead I see a balcony. It's the end of winter. I don't go out much. Yesterday it rained. Today it's snowing. When I close my eyes, flashes of light cause pink, peach, salmon and lilac spots to dance on my eyelids.

## April 6

The clouds move slowly. No houses, no trees. Just, to my right, a long building and its shadow stretching over the brown snow. The sky begins to darken. I don't notice anyone around.

## *May 18*

The rain has just stopped. Against the window, transparent drops make the outside big, like magnifying glasses. Through them, the sky is rounded, buildings blurred.

Further north, close to the church with the blue roof, is the fitness centre where I work. I don't see it right now, but I know that at this time of day, because of the activity inside, the fog is beginning to rise on the windows, that between seven and eight o'clock the heat and humidity are at their peak, the outside gradually withdraws, dissolves like a dream.

## May 21

Since the demolition of the shed, last November, all that is left in the yard is a single tree. On the lowest branch, I see new leaves, still wrinkled. Six of them sway in a ray of light. A gust of wind turns over the second one. After that, my attention flags and I stop counting. The details recede. The tree with its thin branches appears to me whole. It moves slowly like seaweed, ripples in the liquid heat. Its movement mesmerizes me. It is not a tree at all.

## August 15

Last fall my cat disappeared. One evening, as usual, I opened the door to let her out. The hours passed. I started waiting for her. She never came home. I never knew if she was dead, injured, or if she was simply lost. During the time following her disappearance, I became very aware of the sounds around me. Especially the cries of gulls that I associated, when they came from afar, with her meow. Those cries would give me hope, each time disappointed. Afterwards, the void created by her absence seemed larger and larger.

Today I'm sitting on my balcony, exposed to the warm breath of the wind. Although I no longer hope, I still can't free myself of that waiting: watching for Inchauspé's return has become a kind of tic. High in the sky, under the pale sun, gulls make slow turns. They are all hovering at different heights. Drawn up by the air currents, they sometimes let themselves fall, follow each other for a moment, then return to altitude. Every time I hear their feeble cries, I have to convince myself not to look around. I continue squinting at the sky.

## *July 13*

It's at the end of the street, in the opening between the trees, that the yellow of the sky is the brightest. Cars tow long shadows behind them. It's raining. Pollen, not yet weighed down by the rain, floats in the air. The windows of buildings, the windows of cars, all closed, give me a feeling of being absolutely alone. For a moment, I think of nothing, I wait for nothing. There is the yellow sky, the flakes of pollen, the black shadows of the windows.

## *July 23*

The sky above the roofs is only a line. Day is just beginning to break. The rectangles of grass in front of the buildings are bathed in a bluish light. Why is it at this time, in front of this section of the street, that I remember after so many years the taste of methylene blue? My soles scrape the sidewalk.

## November 20

Leaning against a brick building, I look at the trees, grey and bare before me. They aren't beautiful trees. Since this morning, the sky has been covered in an even white.

## February 19

The rain falls almost noiselessly on the snow. On the sill of the slightly open window, water accumulates. Everything is drab outside. No glare from the snow. The metal of the stairs doesn't shine.

# This Could Be Anywhere

## November 28

The furniture, the plant, the big pot at the back of the kitchen. With the backlighting, everything looks black and on the same plane. If I don't interpret reality, on the table in front of me there is a plant growing with a leaf the shape of a pot.

## January 4

I dreamed last night that a fly landed on the inside of a windshield. Behind it, the road, the trees, the wells streamed by. After travelling what seemed like a hundred kilometres, I parked the car and opened the door. The fly, which had stayed on the same spot until then, simply flew away. A black point above the waves that vanished immediately. I woke up with these questions: does a fly feel at home anywhere? In a day, does it retrace the same routes? Can I even imagine the possibility of a life without attachment?

## *January 29*

End of January. It's raining. I bring my cheek close to the coolness of the glass. On the street, the snow is breaking up and trickling everywhere.

# January 20

The trees stay bent. The wind never eases enough for them to regain their verticality. It carries off the snow, which accumulates on the windowsill, darkening the room. If I look away, stare at the bottom of the wall, my feet, the work table, I still hear the wind.

## January 14

Between the branches, the sun still radiates weakly. I take small steps across the ice. The skating rink is deserted. I bring my hands close to my face. They smell like rope. I'm starving.

# *January 8*

A dime touches the snow and digs a hole. Where does this need to pick it up come from?

# January 20

When I walk past the bedroom door, a particular experience of clouds often comes to mind. I was sitting in the backseat of a car. I think it was summer. There was nothing exceptional about the clouds that day, but their shadows could be seen running everywhere: over the fields, the barns and the houses when there were any, over the patches of melting snow (so it wasn't summer). The grasses along the road dazzled as they streamed by, and sometimes cars lined up on the shoulder pulled out. The image stayed with me. Imprecise and finally quite ordinary. With no connection to the door of the room. My head, in my memory, was resting on a pillow.

# February 19

Because of the dim light, the white walls look grey. Piles of dishes were left on the counter, but the food doesn't seem to be in a mess. Thomas slides a hand up my back then pulls it away. My sweater stays pushed up. On my skin, I feel the air moving.

## *March 17*

On the wall, between the shelf with the plants and the television, shines the outline of a hand too wide to be mine. The sun now falls directly on it. In fact, you can see only half the hand. Not the palm, nor the thumb or index finger. The print has been there for years. With time, it has become a subtle decoration, which I connect with nothing and which I don't notice all the time.

## March 24

The streets go by one after the other, barely different. In a window, a few pots of coriander.

## April 11

On the phone, Julie tells me about her holiday at the seashore. I imagine a grey beach, huge waves. For a short time, and yet a long time, Julie's voice is lost. The sounds around her put pressure on my temples, as if my head were submerged in water.

# *May 2*

This happens to me every spring. What's my age? What month is it? Spontaneously, I'm not able to remember.

## April 21

I move away from the window and go back to sit at the table. The kind of afternoon when you'd like to withdraw from everything, clear your mind, become a cup, not think about anything, stay in the same place until evening, absent.

# May 2

Thomas puts down the straw he's been smoothing between his fingers all morning. The daylight behind him obscures his face, his neck.

## April 11

The shadows of the room now extend over the floor and the wall, which deflects them. Watching them, I realize simply, without any seriousness, that I'm not overly fond of life.

## *March 22*

The glass is sitting in the usual place. Same thing for the socks at the foot of the couch, and the book. Three objects sitting on the pale floor, almost at equal distances. If right now I dwell on them, it's not because they bother me. Nor because I attach any importance to them. Objects, like landscapes, exist around me without any more worth than that. They don't give me any meaning. But sharing them with you does.

## *May 24*

It may be the same elsewhere. A door that doesn't close properly. An empty wall. At the end of a table, a not very high plant. The smell of ripe bananas. Grains of dust. A paper.

## *June 21*

Under the railing of the balcony hangs a rope, white and yellow. I look at the sky, the wall, then the rope that the wind is flapping against the wall. The wood is wet and cold. Air enters at the bottom of my clothes. On the shelf attached to the handrail, four jars. One of them is empty and has been overturned by the wind.

# Or Farther Away

You look out the window one day, and you see people walking around with their bags in the rain. You see water spraying from under cars, piles of dead leaves in yards, dark walls. You feel neither sadness, nor joy, nor any other feeling. You just stand there behind the window, watching a street that looks like any other street. People continue passing, cars drive by, but you don't see them anymore. This lasts a few seconds or minutes, and you wouldn't even be able to say what you're thinking. And suddenly, because you're cold, or hungry, or have something to do, you leave the room.

It has nothing to do with boredom. What are the words then for this kind of moment?

You wait on a street corner. You look without actually seeing the beam of light that bounces off the windshield, the puddles. The street stretches on and soon crosses another street. At the far end of a yard, empty chairs.

Standing behind the kitchen counter, or sitting at the table, it doesn't matter. The feeling persists. You gaze through the window, which looks out on another window or on a yard. The brick, the snow: this could be anywhere. Suddenly memories of a place resurface. A very specific place, but you don't know what to connect it to. First you see a wall. In the centre of that wall, a hole plugged with cloth. An aroma of tea in the air and also, more subtly, wet wool. In the left corner of the room, near the kitchen sink, a knife and a glass. Next to the window, a calendar. A feeling that it's early, that there's something missing (something or maybe someone), but you can't say what. Outside, a beam blackened by rain can be seen. Behind, a flooded field. The floor is cold. It looks like the light has dimmed.

A warm breeze. On the counter, an open can of green beans.

# About the Author

Maude Smith Gagnon was born in Basse-Côte-Nord and now lives in Montreal. She has a Master of Arts degree in literary studies from the Université du Québec à Montréal. Her first poetry collection, *Une tonne d'air,* was the winner of the Émile-Nelligan award and her second book, *Un drap. Une place.*, won the 2012 Governor General's Award for French-language poetry.

# About the Translator

Howard Scott was born in southwestern Ontario and moved to Quebec in 1975. His translation of *L'Euguélionne* by Louky Bersianik won the Governor General's Literary Award in 1997. He has translated many poetry, fiction, and non-fiction titles, often in collaboration with Phyllis Aronoff. In 2001, they won the Quebec Writers' Federation Translation Award and in 2009 they were shortlisted for the Governor General's Literary Award. He is a past president of the Literary Translators' Association of Canada. He currently lives in Montreal.